Saint Andrew
for Beginners

Rennie McOwan

First published in 1996 by
SAINT ANDREW PRESS
121 George Street, Edinburgh EH2 4YN

Copyright © Rennie McOwan 1996

ISBN 0 7152 0725 3

British Library Cataloguing in Publication Data
A catalogue record for this book
is available from the British Library.

ISBN 0715207253

Cover design and **internal layout** by Mark Blackadder.
Cover photographs by Walter Bell.
Internal illustrations adapted from 'The Scottish Annals' from Macfarlane & Thomson: *The Comprehensive History of England* (Blackie & Sons, 1861); Miller: *Scripture History* (1840); Green: *Scottish Pictures* (Religious Tract Society, 1891).
Typesetting in Helvetica and Bembo by Lesley Ann Taylor.
Printed and **bound** in Great Britain by Bell & Bain Ltd, Glasgow.

Saint Andrew
for Beginners

Contents

For
AGNES
with gratitude and love

Dedication

SPECIAL thanks are due to
The Rev. MAXWELL CRAIG
The Rev. CHARLES EDIE
ANNE CLAVEIROLE
LIBBY URQUHART
TOM McOWAN
RONALD PATON
JAMES S ADAM

Acknowledgments

Saint Andrew
A Man for God

WHEN the Scottish football team runs out on to the pitch at Hampden Park in Glasgow, or the Scottish rugby team appears at Murrayfield Stadium in Edinburgh, they will be wearing blue jerseys. We all *cheer* them!

Why is the colour blue used?

The choice of this colour is not an accident. Blue, or dark-blue, has become 'the Scottish colour' for other sports as well – like hockey and athletics, and even for the Scottish team who play American Football – the Scottish Claymores.

Blue is the colour of the sky and the choice of that colour for the country of Scotland is based on an old legend or tale.

Part of this story has also helped to give the people of Scotland their own flag. It has a white or silver 'X'-shaped cross on a blue background and it is called the 'Saltire'. You can find out more about the Saltire later in this book.

This is all part of the story of Saint Andrew – the Patron Saint of Scotland. [Sometimes you will see the word 'Saint' appear in print as 'St' – that is just a short way of spelling it, an abbreviation.] The word 'Patron' means that Andrew is very special and Scottish people like to think that Saint Andrew looks after them in a very special way. So the Scots respect and honour him.

But *who* is Andrew, and *what* is a 'saint'?

Let us start at the beginning.

★ ★ ★

Scotland is a mainly Christian country. Most people believe that a wonderful God exists, who created all the world and the universe, and who looks after all that he created, and who loves us all.

But God gave you and me something called 'free will', and when we use our free will, we can use it to love God, or we can use it to ignore God or to say 'no' to him.

We can try to be kind and helpful to other people, or we can be cruel and selfish.

In other words, we can choose to do what we like. It may be good or it may be bad – but we can choose.

God could have made us like little puppets with no freedom of will or choice, but God did not do that. God so loved his people that he gave us freedom to choose how we behave. That is a great gift.

Christians believe that 2000 years ago God came into the lives of people on this planet Earth in a special way. It changed the history of the world.

It can be very hard for us to understand exactly what happened at that time. God can do anything, but we human beings cannot and so it is sometimes difficult to understand what God is up to. The clever men and women who try to explain these things are called 'theologians'. This long word comes from the Greek language – *theo* meaning 'God' and *logos* meaning 'to teach' or 'to talk about'.

God wants human beings to be kind and loving. When people eventually die on this earth, God wants them to live with him for-ever in a place of total happiness. That place is called 'Heaven'.

So God came down to the Earth in the form of a person. That person is God's Son, and he is called Jesus Christ.

The word 'Jesus' is simply a name – like David or Tracey or Ross. The word 'Christ', however, comes from a Greek word, *Christos*, meaning 'the anointed one'. [Special people long ago had scented oil rubbed on them as a sign of reverence and respect.]

It is a bit difficult to understand, but Jesus Christ was also God as well. But, more than that – Jesus' *love* for people and the *help* or *power*

God gave Jesus to say and do wonderful things during his time on the Earth, we call the 'Holy Spirit' or the 'Holy Ghost'.

So in fact we have three Persons in the one God – yet they are all still the One God.

Christians call this belief 'The Trinity' – meaning 'three'. It means that *God the Father* (creator of the world), *God the Son* (Jesus Christ) and *God the Holy Spirit,* are separate and yet one. And all are truly God in a way we can only guess at.

★   ★   ★

Now Jesus was born in a country called Palestine, which today is part of, or close to, modern Israel. In Jesus' time it was part of the Roman Empire. People today call it the Holy Land.

Jesus loved all people and tried to look after them, to find them food when they were hungry, or to cure them of illness or disease. When he was an adult, Jesus travelled around the countryside, caring for and helping people in need.

He was helped by other people. His very special band of twelve helpers were called the 'Disciples', or 'Apostles'. These followers became known as 'Christians'. The word 'apostle' comes from a Greek word which means 'sent' – someone who brings a message. It also represents the person sending the message. The word 'disciple' means someone who believes in the teachings of another person.

Jesus trained his Disciples (Apostles) to help him as he worked among the poor and needy. He also wanted them to keep on loving and caring for people in need after he died. So they would have to learn from their Master very carefully. This was important work.

The Disciples were the first 'Christians', followers of Jesus Christ. They set up the Christian Church almost twenty centuries ago.

★ ★ ★

A terrible thing happened to Jesus. But although it was terrible, it also had a *wonderful* effect on the whole world – an effect which can still be felt today.

Some of the people who lived at the same time as Jesus, knew of him and hated him. Why? After all, huge crowds of folk flocked to Jesus for help and sometimes he provided food for them or cured people in a way they thought was like magic. These were his 'miracles' – and most of the people thought *he* was brilliant, wonderful, magic!

But other people, people in power, thought Jesus was getting too powerful himself. They thought he might be a threat to the Romans who ruled the Holy Land at that time.

And the leaders of other faiths and religions were envious of Jesus' popularity with all the folk. They thought that the people were not paying as much attention to them as they once did. Not only that, but Jesus sometimes spoke against the leaders. Jesus thought that these people in power were not kind enough to those that they led.

So Jesus was put in prison. He was beaten and then killed. He was executed in a very cruel way.

First a crown of thorns was placed upon his head – because his enemies said that he had pretended to be a king so he should have a crown. Then he was nailed to a wooden structure shaped like a cross, with nails through his hands and feet. He was left to die.

This terrible method of execution was called 'crucifixion', from the Latin word which means 'a cross'. A cross was often used to execute criminals in the time of Jesus. People were used to seeing wrong-doers and criminals killed in this way – and so it was not unusual.

But another event took place which *was* unusual – which changed the world.

Because Jesus died …

But then he rose from the dead.

He came alive again!

Jesus left his grave, his tomb – some of his friends *actually* saw him – before he joined God the Father in Heaven.

And because of this wonderful event, this Miracle of *all* miracles, Jesus Christ still lives for Christians today in a very real way. He is still with them in their minds and hearts and in the ways he can help them to live good lives.

By doing all this, Jesus was giving his followers a message. By *choosing* to die – when he could have escaped – he was showing his love for everyone.

He was making up for all the bad things in the world.

He was making a sacrifice of himself for the sake of others.

By choosing to die, by accepting a horrible death, he made certain that his followers, too, can go to Heaven.

Jesus made it clear by his action that God *does* love everyone. He made it plain that God wants folk to love God in return. And God wants us to try to make a better world here on earth, as well as looking forward to Heaven.

★   ★   ★

The act of Jesus rising from the dead is called the 'Resurrection'. That long word comes from Latin and means 'to rise again' or 'new life'.

The *Birth* of Jesus Christ is celebrated at Christmas time.

The *Resurrection* of Jesus Christ is celebrated at Easter.

★ ★ ★

After the death and resurrection of Jesus Christ, his followers began to travel far and wide, and mostly on foot, to spread his wonderful message of love all over the world.

The Cross stopped being merely a terrible and ugly form of execution. It became a sign of hope, and love, and of caring.

For example, you may have heard of the 'Red Cross'? It is an organisation which was set up to help sick people, those injured in accidents and those affected by tragedy. The symbol ✚ is used for the Red Cross and there are many other examples of the Cross being used these days as a special sign of hope for people.

★ ★ ★

What we have said so far will set the scene for our introduction to Saint Andrew.

Andrew was a Christian. In fact, Andrew was a *Disciple* or *Apostle* of Jesus Christ himself and he was one of the first to follow the Master.

In the next chapter, you will learn more about Andrew's story.

NOTE

The format of this book has been designed in such a way as to help the reader understand the main aspects of the background to the life of Saint Andrew. Questions, Things to Do, Information Panels and Follow-up Exercises are features of this book.

THE APOSTLES

The twelve *Disciples* or *Apostles* chosen by Jesus to help him in his work are called:

SIMON – also known as Peter

JOHN – the son of a fisherman

JAMES the GREATER – a brother of John

ANDREW – brother of Simon Peter

PHILIP

BARTHOLOMEW – also called Peter

MATTHEW – a tax collector

THOMAS – known as 'doubting Thomas' because he did not believe at first that Jesus had come back from the dead

JAMES the LESS

JUDE

SIMON – not Simon Peter

JUDAS

THE BIBLE

Christian people use a special book in their lives and their worship in church. It is called the Bible. Here are some facts about the Bible:

- The word 'Bible' comes from a Greek word which means 'the Book'.
  The Bible is a kind of library. It is made up of letters, stories, bits of history, personal tales, prayers, song words, important documents and eye-witness accounts of the life of Jesus Christ.
- The Bible is divided into two parts:
  Part 1 – The Old Testament – is mainly a history of the Jewish people. It sets the scene for the birth of Jesus Christ.
  Part 2 – The New Testament – is mainly an account of the life of Jesus Christ and it is divided into sections. Some of these sections are called 'Gospels', from a word which means 'joyful' or 'good news'.
  Some of the Disciples were thought to have written some of these sections – for example, the Gospel of John. And some of *their* friends also wrote down what they remembered about Jesus – for example, the Gospel of Luke.

THINGS TO DO

- How many Books are there in the New Testament?
  Can you learn the order in which they appear?
- Do you know the stories of any of Jesus' miracles?
  Draw a picture of one of them. There are many miracles to choose from.
  [How about the one with the five loaves and two fish which has something to do with Andrew! See pages 18 and 19 of this book.]
- Look up a map of the world to find where modern Palestine and Israel are?
- Draw and colour in a picture of the strips of the Scottish football and/or rugby teams?
- The symbol ✚ is used for the Red Cross.
  Can you think of any other examples of the Cross being used today as a special sign of caring for people?

CHAPTER 1

Andrew's Story

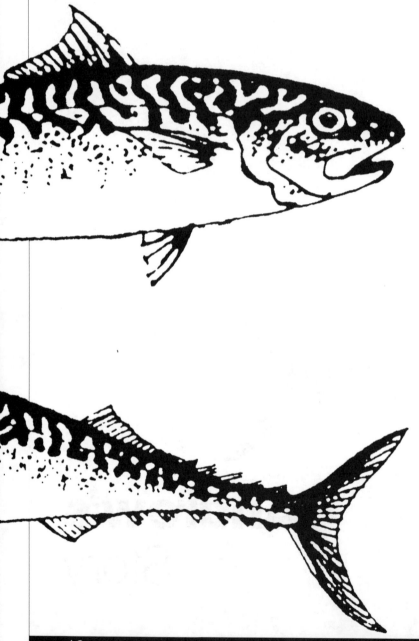

WE can find out a lot about the life of Andrew from the Bible. We first meet him when we are told that Andrew once saw a man called John 'the Baptist', who was a preacher and a 'prophet'. A 'prophet' is a man or a woman who can tell what is going to happen in the future.

John the Baptist told the people who had come to listen to him preach that there was a man called Jesus Christ who was *truly* the Son of God. He urged people to follow the teachings of this man. Andrew was in that crowd and he heard John's message.

★ ★ ★

One of the best known sections of the Bible is the Gospel written by Mark. He reports that one day a man called Jesus was walking by the Sea of Galilee, in the Holy Land.

There Jesus saw Simon and his brother *Andrew* fishing with a casting net. They did not use rods and lines, but a net which they dragged through the water.

Jesus then said a very strange thing to Simon and Andrew – something that was to change *their* lives and the lives of thousands upon thousands of people after that day.

Jesus said: 'Come with me and I will make you *fishers of men*.'

And so Simon and Andrew left their nets and followed Jesus. They became his first chosen *Disciples*.

★ ★ ★

Simon and Andrew were so excited about the things Jesus taught them that they felt his wonderful teaching about Heaven and how God loved people should be told to other people.

They thought that Jesus' wish that people should love one another should be taught to as many folk as possible.

So the two Disciples became close friends of Jesus. They became 'fans' of Jesus, as we would say nowadays. They became his helpers, his supporters. And they in turn became teachers, talking to crowds of people in the open air, preaching the message the Master had taught them.

Simon and Andrew were prepared to leave their work as fishermen to help Jesus, because they had never met anyone quite like him before. But if you think about it, perhaps it was just like fishing after all, gathering *people* in, becoming 'fishers of men'. Yes, they were happy doing this and so were the people they 'caught'.

Five Loaves and Two Fish

The Gospel written by John tells us that Andrew was the man who helped those who wanted to meet Jesus and to hear him speak. He took them into the presence of Jesus.

John tells of one particular occasion when Jesus was speaking to a very large crowd. More and more people kept arriving at the spot because they had heard that Jesus had been *curing* ill people.

The crowd soon numbered over *five thousand.*

A lot of the people who came to hear Jesus were poor. Many had travelled over long distances. Many had no food. They were tired and hungry.

Just as the problem seemed to be getting out of hand, Andrew bumped into a small boy among the crowd. He had five loaves made of barley, and two silvery fish.

Andrew told Jesus about the boy's lunch, but he did not think it would be of much use to the folk who were, by now, *really* hungry.

But Jesus simply asked all the people to sit down and then he said a short prayer, a prayer of a kind which is often said before meals. It is called a 'grace'.

Jesus then began to break up the boy's loaves and fish and pass the food around.

A strange thing happened. *There was enough food for everybody.*

It was as if the amount of food had grown and grown.

And not only did the whole crowd eat and eat until they were full, but there were enough pieces left over to fill twelve large baskets.

Some people read about this event and believe that Jesus used his special power to make the loaves and fish grow in number. They call something like this, something puzzling, where something apparently impossible happens, a 'miracle'.

Jesus, the Son of God, had the power to make this happen.

But other people believe that when people saw Jesus and the boy being generous and sharing out the small meal of bread and fish, this had a good effect on other people. Some of the people who had brought their own food, and who were selfishly hugging it to themselves, grew a bit ashamed.

They were sorry for being selfish. They were sorry for being greedy so they shared their food with other people.

This meant that *everyone* got something to eat.

But whether Jesus did work a miracle that day, or whether his example made other people wish to do what he had done – the end result was the same. For the people who were hungry were *all* given food enough to eat. Wasn't that great?

Jesus did this wonderful thing and it was Andrew who helped him.

QUESTIONS

– To read about Andrew in the Bible, look up these examples:

John	chapter	1	verses 35 to 42
John	chapter	6	verses 1 to 15
John	chapter	12	verses 20 to 26

– Do you think that Jesus really did work a miracle with the five barley loaves and two small fish?

– When the people had eaten their fill, there were twelve baskets of left-overs? What do you think happened to them?

Jesus and Andrew must have been very happy to see everyone with food enough to satisfy their hunger.

– If you watch the news on the television, you may have heard of the aid agencies that exist today – like Oxfam, Christian Aid, War on Want, the Save the Children Fund, the Scottish Catholic International Aid Fund, and many others – which try to provide food for people overseas who do not have enough, and to help people who are in need in our own land.

They try to help people to grow more food.

They help provide medicine, hospitals and schools.

So you see, Jesus' great example of helping people who are poor or in need still goes on today. We can all help these agencies to help other people – just as Andrew did.

THINGS TO DO

- Design a large, colourful poster for one of the Aid agencies. You could put the small boy into the poster, with his loaves and fish.
- Or make a model of Simon and his brother Andrew trying to catch fish with a net on the Sea of Galilee. Use cardboard for the boat and string for the net.
- Or draw the scene of the fishermen hard at work on the Sea of Galilee. Try to imagine what the scene might be like. Remember that the men would be wearing very different clothes from fishermen today and the boats would be very different too.

   Or you may wish to make a drawing which shows Jesus calling Simon and Andrew to follow him.
- You could make a large frieze of the crowd which shared the loaves and fish with Jesus. You could cut the figures out of magazines and build up the picture. Don't forget to feature Jesus, Andrew and, of course, the little boy who provided the food. He would probably have been around primary school age. It must have been a great shock to him when *everybody* got a bit of his lunch to eat that day.

Telling the Good News

After the death of Jesus, Andrew is believed to have travelled to a country called Greece. He went there to pass on the teachings of Jesus – the 'Good News' – to people far away beyond the Holy Land.

To do this Andrew must have been a very brave man for there were some people who were afraid of the early Christians, the followers of Jesus Christ. They thought that those people who gathered crowds of folk together to hear about the work of Jesus were just stirring up trouble.

The Christians were thought to be enemies of the powerful Romans, whose Empire spread across many lands, because the Christians said that Jesus Christ was more important than any-one else on earth.

The Christians sometimes said that other religions were untrue and false, and this also turned some people against them.

The Christians also told people not to hate their enemies, but to *love* them. That shocked some people, for they had been brought up to hate their enemies and to kill them. Why would they want to *love* them?

But Andrew and his friends kept going. They were filled with a tremendous energy. They were very happy and enthusiastic. They loved what they were doing.

They totally believed that Jesus Christ was truly God, as well as being a human person.

They wanted people to love God. They wanted people to love one another. They wanted people to go to Heaven.

They wanted to end cruelty and badness on earth.

They wanted to tell *everyone* about Jesus!

They were very brave men and women who were prepared to be killed by their enemies, rather than turn back. And they were determined to speak out for what they believed at all times.

Andrew's Death

What fate befell Andrew?

Poor, brave Andrew was murdered.

He is believed to have been killed at a place in Greece called Patras.

Like Jesus, he was killed in a very cruel way. He was *crucified* by his enemies.

Some people believe that the Cross which Andrew was nailed to was a different shape from the one used for Jesus' death – it was shaped like the letter 'X'. It later became known as 'St Andrew's Cross'. It also became known as 'the Saltire', from words in the Old French language, which in Latin is *crux decussata* – which means a cross shaped like an 'X'. It is also thought that Saint Andrew may have been crucified upside down.

This Saltire shape was to become the design of the Scottish flag.

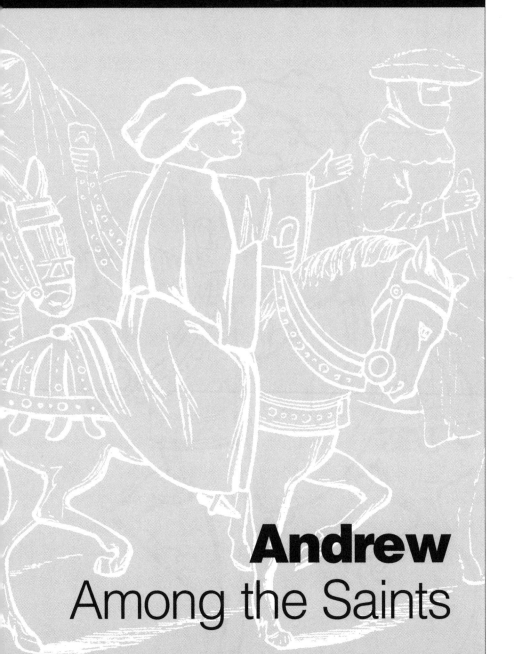

CHAPTER 2

Andrew
Among the Saints

ANDREW

is a saint, the Patron Saint of Scotland. We call him 'Saint Andrew'. But what *is* a 'saint'? What do we mean when we say a man or a woman is a 'saint'.

With Peter, James and John, Andrew's name is among the first to appear on the list of Apostles, those very special friends of Jesus.

Let us now look at what we already know about Andrew:
—   He was a fisherman, and he was the brother of Simon Peter.
—   The father of Andrew and Simon Peter was called Jona. He was a fisherman from Galilee, in the Holy Land.
—   Andrew is thought to have been born in a place called Bethsaida and to have lived and worked as a fisherman in a place called Capernaum.
—   Andrew's desire to become a Christian is reported very early on in the sections of the Bible we call the Gospels.
—   He may have introduced Simon Peter to Jesus.

How does all this make Andrew a 'saint'?
—   A saint is a very kind person, who tries to help other people.
—   A saint is a person who tries to love God.
—   A saint is a person who tries to stay cheerful in bad times.
—   A saint is a person who tries to be brave in the face of cruel enemies.
—   A saint is a person who tries to be patient and not get angry with other people.
—   A saint is a person who makes loving God and other people the most important thing in his or her life.

Is Andrew all these things?

★ ★ ★

The word 'saint' comes from the Latin word *sanctus,* meaning 'holy'.
Saints are very nice people. They don't have to be stern-faced or
serious all the time. In fact, lots of people we call saints are, or were,
very happy people. They liked to laugh. They were filled with joy.

★ ★ ★

People who have been very brave in times of war are sometimes
given medals. The most important British medal of all is called the
'Victoria Cross', first awarded by Queen Victoria in 1856. A similar
medal is given to very brave people who are caught up in a war,
although not actually fighting in it like soldiers – to 'civilians', in
other words. It is called the 'George Cross' (named after King George
VI and first awarded in 1940).

The Victoria Cross is called the 'V.C.' for short.

When we hear that somebody has been awarded the Victoria
Cross or the George Cross, we know that this person is very special
indeed. Everyone knows that they have been very brave. Everyone
knows that the person is a hero or a heroine. We look up to them. We
admire them. We want to be like them.

Saints are like 'V.C.s'. They are the medal-winners of the Church.
They are our heroes. They are our heroines. They have shown courage
and patience. They have put other people before themselves.

They have tried to love God, and tried to care for other people.

They are examples for us to follow. They are very special people.
And anyone can be like them if they want to be.

Early Christians

In the Bible the word 'saint' is used to describe all Christians. That means they were followers of Jesus Christ. His special love changed their lives.

The early Christian followers were small in number. The Christian Church in the modern world now numbers millions of people and is represented in *every* part of the world. That is an amazing fact.

Nowadays we tend only to use the word 'saint' for very special people, for heroic people, for outstanding Christians.

Andrew is called a 'saint', a special follower of Christ. He is a hero, a brave man, an example for us all to follow.

He is one of the 'V.C.s' of the Church.

Before we find out why Andrew is so special in Scotland, we have to look at how the Church today regards 'saints'.

This is very important when we come to understand why Saint Andrew is not just a saint, but Scotland's *Patron* Saint.

Churches in Scotland

In Scotland there are three main Christian Churches. They are the Church of Scotland, the Roman Catholic Church and the Scottish Episcopal Church.

There are also Christians who belong to other Churches in Scotland – like the Baptist Church, Methodist Church, United Reformed Church, Free Church of Scotland, and so on.

These Churches don't always agree with one another when looking at aspects of Christ's life. They don't always agree about how the whole Church of God should be run, or what it should say or do. But they all *do* believe that the Disciples (Apostles) were real people. They all believe that the Disciples were followers of Christ.

They all believe that Andrew was one of the Disciples and that he was a wonderful man. They all call him 'Saint Andrew'.

They all believe that people today should try to love God and should try to be more like the saints.

They all agree Saint Andrew is the Patron Saint of Scotland.

Remembering the Saints

Lots of towns and villages and streets and bridges and hospitals and schools and churches and people's names in Britain today are taken from saints who lived centuries ago.

Take hospitals and schools, for example. Think of the famous St Bartholomew's hospital in London, or St John's school, a name used in several towns throughout the land.

Why is this?

Because the Church in the past was a bit like the 'National Health Service' of its day – it built and staffed hospitals. It also provided education by building and staffing schools.

Today the State provides most of the health care and education in Scotland, although not all of it.

To name a church building or a school or a hospital after a saint is to 'dedicate' that building to the person. It means that the saint is remembered and honoured. It means that the example of the saint should be followed.

★ ★ ★

In the Highlands and other parts of Scotland, there are lots of place names linked to saints like, for example, Columba, who founded a Christian community on the west coast island of Iona. Columba was called *Colum Cille* in the Gaelic language.

Other well-known saints in the Highlands include Saint Bride and Saint Maolrubha. Saint Ninian was one of the first Christian missionaries in Scotland, to the southern part of Scotland in particular.

If you see the word 'Kil-' on a map – such as *Kil*marnock in Ayrshire, or *Kil*martin in Argyll – it often means that a church stood there, or some other building like a monastery where monks lived and worked. The word *kil* comes from the older word *cille* in the Gaelic language.

Sometimes places were named after a saint who actually lived there. Sometimes the church or other building was dedicated to a saint, even though the saint had not ever visited the place.

For example, the old name for the town of Perth was 'St John's toun' (town), named after Saint John, one of the Disciples. That name may not be used for the town today, but there are still signs of it – after all, Perth's football team is called St Johnstone!

Another example of a football team with a saintly background is St Mirren – the team takes its name from a sixth century saint who worked in the area of Paisley and Govan.

★ ★ ★

However, of *all* the churches dedicated to saints in Scotland – and many, many churches are dedicated to saints – Saint Andrew is by far the most popular name.

THINGS TO DO

- Find a detailed street map of a city – like Edinburgh, Glasgow, Newcastle, Birmingham, London or Aberdeen, or your own city or town.
  Can you spot any saints' names on your map? Make a list.
  [Look out for churches and hospitals and bridges and streets, for example.]
- Make a booklet about the life of a saint you have heard of – like Columba, Ninian, Cuthbert, Margaret or Mungo – there are many, many more to choose from. Draw scenes from your chosen saint's life and find out more about the times in which he or she lived.
- Do any of your friends have names which came from the names of saints? For example, what about David or Fergus or Margaret or Bridget? Can you find out more about where these names came from?

Relics

Many Christians long ago liked to own objects which once belonged to a saint. It meant a lot to them.

That should not seem strange to us today. We all keep things which hold happy memories for us – like photographs of people we know, or letters friends have written to us. And we all bring back objects from places where we have had a great holiday – like pens and mugs and key-rings – usually with the name of the holiday place printed on the side. We also keep pictures or cuttings of footballers and pop singers and actors and movie stars. Sometimes people even keep a lock of hair from someone they love.

We call these things 'souvenirs' or 'mementos' or 'memorabilia' because they remind us of something special.

Long ago, people called special objects 'relics'. These relics were not like key-rings or mugs, but rather more unusual kinds of objects – like bits of clothing owned by the saint in question, or pieces of wood which was said to have come from the Cross that Jesus died on. Some Christians in past centuries even kept pieces of bone from the bodies of dead saints.

This might seem strange to some Christians today. They might not like this way of remembering the saints.

But other Christians believe that relics are important. They say that it makes them realise properly that the saints were real people. They weren't just people in stories – so relics of the saints should be treated with great seriousness and devotion.

They say that relics help them to follow the example of the lives of the saints and the life of Jesus. Some believe that relics and the prayers of the saints can help them to pray to God in a much better way.

But other Christians do not believe this. They think that to use relics in such a way is wrong. They say it is a bit like magic – they don't like it and they don't agree with it.

Instead, they want people's prayers to go straight to God and not through the use of a relic to make them remember a saint, by whose example they can follow the teachings of God.

These differences are hard to explain in a few words, but the way people think about relics does play a part in the importance of Saint Andrew as a saint and as the Patron Saint of Scotland.

The Relics of Saint Andrew

Relics of the early saints were once considered very important, but there were some people who told lies about relics. They claimed to have a relic of a saint when it was not real. They pretended that any old object – a piece of ox bone, or a fragment of cloth, or an ornament of some sort – once actually belonged to a saint. These were false relics.

Sometimes relics were sold for money, a terrible thing to do.

Sometimes a city, or an important church, would say it housed a relic of a saint because lots of people would then visit just to see it. This special relic made the city or church feel important and powerful.

Travellers who came to visit the city or church were called 'pilgrims' – from the Latin word *peregrinus,* meaning 'a stranger'. These pilgrims spent lots of money on their travels. It was big business. They also believed that God would show them special favours if they owned a special relic.

Sometimes a relic of a saint was shown to ill people because it was believed it might help them to recover.

Sometimes important people used a relic to protect them against their enemies. They sought God's favour by honouring this relic. The Scottish king Robert the Bruce, for example, wanted the bones of a saint called Fillan carried in front of his army at the Battle of Bannockburn in 1314.

Saint Fillan was a special saint to a lot of people in Scotland at that time, although not a lot is known about him. The King hoped that the sacred relic would help the Scottish army – with the help of God – to defeat the invading army of King Edward II of England.

★ ★ ★

Long ago, some Christians believed, rightly or wrongly, that they actually *owned* parts of the body of Saint Andrew. These bones meant a lot to them and relics of Saint Andrew are still kept in churches in places like Rome, Turkey and Edinburgh even to this day. They can still be seen and examined.

Many other Christians these days do not get very excited about this. They say it is a long time since Saint Andrew died – nearly two thousand years! No one can possibly be sure that these relics are *real*. They might be bogus, they might be nothing at all to do with the Saint himself. Remember what we said about some people in the past lying about the relics being truly what they said they were.

No, some people say, it is wrong to make too much of relics.

These objects should be thought of as historic, but not special. They should not be treated as part of their lives as Christians.

But not all people feel this way. If relics were important in the past, some people believe, then they should still be important to Christians today.

★ ★ ★

Old accounts of the lives of the saints can often seem puzzling to us today. They may have stories or legends mixed up in them. They may have tales of saints working splendid miracles or suffering from terrible tragedies. Some of these stories will make us gasp! Some are a mixture of older stories which people told in the days *before* they heard about Christianity. Some of them are so strange that it is difficult to believe that they ever happened at all.

It sometimes needs a lot of work to sort them out and a lot of study of the different accounts of the story.

People long ago were not like us. Many believed in tales and stories that you and I today might find too ridiculous or fantastic to believe. Some would be true, of course, but some would have bits of the truth mixed up with things which were merely imagined.

To understand why Andrew became an important saint, we have to understand all the stories that are told about him. We have to understand why these Christians in the past believed all these stories and what they thought and did about them.

To do so, let us take time to understand about Christianity and the Church – how it came to exist, and how the teachings of Jesus spread from the Holy Land to many other countries.

THINGS TO DO

- Some churches organise pilgrimages for their own congregation or along with other churches in the area. It can be a great day out.
- Pilgrimages are part of other religions and faiths too – not just the Christian faith. It is good to know about this and to respect it. Find out more about pilgrims and pilgrimages in a faith that is not your own.

  [The Roman Catholic pilgrimage grotto at Carfin, near Motherwell, now has a visitor centre telling the story of pilgrimages in all religions.]
- Draw a picture of a crowd of pilgrims heading towards a holy place – a cave or a church, for example. Your crowd could be full of all different people, young, old, rich, poor, and so on.

  If you are part of a class, each member can draw one pilgrim, cut it out, and build up the crowd scene with all the different pictures.
- Your family or your school could organise an outing to a local site famous for its links with a saint, or to a museum, or an abbey or church of historical interest.

CHAPTER 3

A Short History of the **Celtic Church**

THIS

chapter provides a short history of the Church – the organisation to which Christians belong. It is true that Christians sometimes disagree with each other about *how* the Church was set up all those centuries ago and they may disagree about its history and the form which Christianity took in the many countries it spread to, but let us look here at the Church as it grew in Northern Europe and, in particular, Scotland.

Most scholars agree that in Scotland, long ago, people belonged to the 'Celtic' branch of the Church.

Its members believed all the main things Jesus taught about God and Heaven. Indeed, they were the same as other Christians in other countries in their belief in most of these main things, but in some ways they differed.

The 'Celtic' Church took its name from the peoples and races who lived in different parts of Northern Europe.

These Celts also lived in Scotland, Ireland and Wales and many of the saints names you hear about in Scotland long ago (see page 31) belonged to the Celtic Church.

These communities of Celtic Christians organised themselves in a particular way. Their pattern of administration was often informal. They tended to be self-contained units. Their members included scholars and artists and experts in healing. Their craftsmen and women produced beautiful Celtic art, including stone carvings and 'illuminated', hand-painted, manuscripts and Celtic knot designs.

Their Church leaders were called *abbots* and *bishops.*

Christians in other countries had different ways of controlling and running the affairs of their Church:

– They had areas of local control – *dioceses.*
  Each diocese was headed by a *bishop.*

- A very important *diocese* was called an *archdiocese*. It was led by an *archbishop*.
- Sometimes a number of *dioceses* were grouped together.
- The most important *bishop* of all was based in Rome, Italy. He became known as the *Pope,* from the Latin *papa,* meaning 'father'. [A very famous saint – Peter – the leader of Jesus' Apostles, was believed to have been crucified in Rome and to have been buried there. Christians who are Roman Catholics believe he was the first Pope.]

★　★　★

As time moved on, the old patterns and ways of life of the Celtic Church changed. The early Celtic Church in Northern Europe was not divided into areas called *dioceses,* but as the Church grew these areas of local control were set up to run the Church more easily.

The use of *dioceses* headed by *bishops* began to spread. It became the normal pattern in many countries and it finally took over the Celtic Church. It absorbed the Celtic Church and changed its character.

Most Christians today in Scotland consider the Celtic Church to be an important part of their own history. They may not always agree which parts of the old Church were good or which were bad, but they are very proud of its heritage.

It is part of their history, their 'pedigree' or 'ancestry', going right back to the time of Jesus.

Today the Church of Scotland, the Roman Catholic Church and the Scottish Episcopal Church all believe that the old Celtic Church had much to tell its members. For the Celtic Church brought such famous names to Scotland and Britain as Columba, who founded a community of monks on the west coast island of Iona – as well as such worthy individuals as Aidan, Cuthbert and Ninian. Its followers created such wonderful pieces of carving and art and books – like the famous *Book of Kells*, or the carved stone crosses that can still be seen. The Celtic Church helped people to see God's wonderful hand in nature in many parts of Scotland.

When *dioceses* and *bishops* became more important to the Celtic Church, the way the Church was run became the same as everywhere else.

Each *diocese* then had a church – the leading church of that *diocese*. These leading churches were called *cathedrals*. The name 'cathedral' comes from a Greek word *cathedra* meaning 'chair', because bishops often sat in a special chair at important meetings of the Church, or when they were teaching people about Christianity. These special chairs were kept inside the most important church in the diocese.

One of the meanings of the word 'city' is a place where there is a cathedral. Of course, we think of a city these days as a great sprawl of buildings, covering many miles, where thousands of people live. We are used to calling such big places 'cities'. But, strictly speaking, a city should have a cathedral.

And so, because of this, some small places in Scotland today are called cities, although most of us today would wonder why. Dunkeld in Perthshire, for example, or St Andrews in Fife – these are cities. Why? Because they have their own cathedrals.

★　★　★

Now the background is set for an explanation of why Saint Andrew is the Patron Saint of Scotland. In the next chapter we shall look at the importance of relics to the story of Andrew's special relationship with Scotland.

CHAPTER 4

Saint Andrew
Relics and Ruins

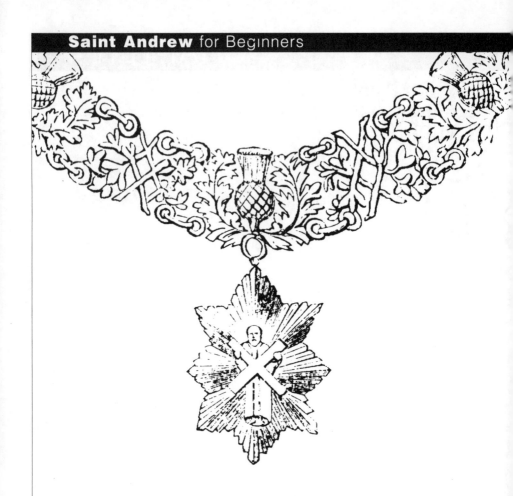

WE have already said that people long ago liked the idea of a church building or a Christian community housing its very own relic or relics of saints (see pages 34 to 35). Remember, a 'relic' is a memento linked to a saint, like a lock of hair or a piece of clothing or a fragment of bone. A relic made people think that the place where it was housed was very important and the visitor hoped that the saint's relics would make God look at them with favour. He or she believed that the relic was evidence that saints were real people and not legends. They hoped the relic would bring them good fortune or prevent illness or cure a disease. And, as we have mentioned earlier, sometimes legends and tales of saints got mixed up over the years with accounts of the *real* life of the saints.

Indeed, it was one such story that resulted in Saint Andrew becoming the Patron Saint of Scotland. This is how it goes.

★ ★ ★

One very old story tells how the bones or relics of Saint Andrew were carried by a man called Saint Regulus (known also as Rule) to the shores of Fife many centuries ago. No one is quite sure of the precise date.

It was a difficult voyage and the ship bearing Regulus was forced to land because of a great storm. Some people say that God created the storm to help Saint Regulus land on that very spot; but others say it is all a story – exciting, but not true.

The story goes on to tell us that Saint Andrew's bones were buried by Regulus at a place called Kirymont. The great cathedral of St Andrew was later built upon that very spot. It became a very important building and its ruins can still be seen today.

★ ★ ★

However, the old Celtic Church in those days also had important centres at Dunkeld, in Perthshire, and Abernethy on the north side of the Ochils. The monks who lived there were called 'Culdees'. This name comes from the Latin words *cultores dei*, or Irish Gaelic words, meaning 'servants of God'.

The Church began to feel that these monastic communities needed tighter control, better management. So they became part of the new structure we talked of earlier – the *dioceses*.

Now, when the great cathedral of St Andrew was built, people thought it was *very* important. They truly believed that Saint Regulus had brought Saint Andrew's relics there, as the story says.

Excited by the great importance of the cathedral of St Andrew, thousands of pilgrims travelled to St Andrews, the city, to see the new cathedral and to marvel at the wondrous relics. The pilgrims brought money and gifts to the area and the modern city of St Andrews and its great cathedral became very important.

In the eleventh century, at the time of Queen Margaret of Scotland, a ferry took pilgrims across the River Forth so that they could travel to St Andrews.

Queen Margaret was a devout Christian who led a good life and was very kind to ordinary people. She herself was to become a saint.

And it was the Queen herself who ordered that a ferry be set up to help the pilgrims. Although the pilgrims took lots of money to St Andrews, they were allowed to travel free on the ferry if they were *actually* pilgrims and not just travellers looking for a free trip!

The ferry gave its name to modern North and South Queensferry, which lie beneath the great road and rail bridges on both sides of the River Forth.

★ ★ ★

Now, as we have said, not everyone thinks that the story of Saint Regulus is true. Some historians say that Saint Regulus was actually a man who lived much earlier in Ireland. But whatever the truth, people long ago *did* believe that there *was* a saint called Saint Regulus. They believed that he did bring the relics of Saint Andrew to the Fife coast and that he was washed ashore in a storm.

They believed the relics of Saint Andrew were true and genuine.

An old tower still stands beside the ruins of the cathedral and is named after Saint Regulus. A cave in the cliffs is reputed to be where Regulus went to find peace and quiet to pray.

THINGS TO DO

- Draw Saint Regulus (Saint Rule) being washed ashore on the coast of Fife, or draw Regulus in his cave.
- How many cathedrals in Scotland can you name?
  Can you find any pictures or photographs of Scottish cathedrals in history books. Draw what you find.
- You could make a model of Queen Margaret's ferry, taking pilgrims across the River Forth in the days when there were no road and rail bridges?
- Find out as much as you can about the city of St Andrews in Fife. For example, what is it famous for? [*Hint:* it is famous for a sport – but *which* sport?]
  What buildings will you find there?
  Is it a big place or a small place? How many people live there?
- You could make up a travel brochure about the city of St Andrews, or your own city, or town or village.
  You can find out more details about your chosen place from old history books. Write the details down in a list.
  Then gather some free tourist leaflets or local maps or travel magazines and cut out the pictures. [*Remember:* make sure you get permission before you cut anything out of a book or magazine.]
  You will need a scrap-book to stick all your work in.
  Arrange it in an attractive way with lots of colour and bold headlines.

Another Legend of Saint Andrew

The relics of Saint Andrew may have been brought to St Andrews in another way. There is more than one legend as to how it happened. The story of Saint Regulus is the best known, but it is not the only one. Here is another story or legend.

Long ago, there was an important abbey at a place called Hexham in Northumberland, which is in the North of England.

The abbey had a famous abbot. (An 'abbot' is the title given to the monk who is in charge of the other monks in the abbey.) This Abbot was called Wilfred.

Wilfred was a very good person and he was to become a saint. He founded two abbeys – one at Hexham and the other at a place called Ripon in Yorkshire. He named Ripon Abbey after Saint Peter, the first Apostle, and he named Hexham after Saint Andrew, Peter's brother.

A very famous writer and historian called The Venerable Bede, who died in the eighth century, wrote in his great history book of the Church that Wilfred was followed as Abbot of Hexham by another man called Acca.

Wilfred and Acca once journeyed to Rome in Italy together – like pilgrims. It was a very long, dangerous journey, mostly on foot. Why did they go there? Because Rome had become a very famous centre for Christianity since people believed that Saint Peter himself was buried there. Rome was an important place for pilgrims.

When they came home again, Wilfred and Acca brought back from Rome relics of famous saints. The people back home marvelled at these relics. They treated them with great respect – they believed that they were proof that the early saints were *real* people.

And it was Acca who gave the reigning Scottish king at that

time – Angus MacFergus – some precious relics of Saint Andrew.

These small pieces of bone and other objects were often kept in specially made, richly ornamented cases or holders called reliquaries. If you visit the Royal Museum of Scotland in Queen Street, Edinburgh, you can see examples of reliquaries from long ago. Some Roman Catholic churches in Scotland still have reliquaries. The Catholic cathedral of St Mary in Edinburgh has a reliquary which is thought to contain some pieces of bone from Saint Andrew's body.

King Angus MacFergus ruled over the ancient peoples of Scotland – the Picts and Scots – from the year AD 820-834. [The letters 'AD', from the Latin *anno Domini,* means 'in the year of our Lord'.]

The word 'Picts' means 'painted people'. When the Roman army invaded Scotland from the South in AD 79 or 80, they gave the fierce native tribes they found there this name, because the people covered their faces and bodies with war-paint and tattoos. We still use the term 'Picts' today when we refer to these ancient tribes.

The Scots race, however, also originally came from Ireland. The Scots and the Picts eventually became one nation – the country now called Scotland.

King Angus MacFergus was delighted with the relics given to him by Acca. They meant a lot to him. He thought the relics would help him to be a better king in the eyes of his people. He thought the relics would help him defeat his enemies.

True enough, he did win a very important battle and he believed that it was Saint Andrew who helped him – through the relics that were brought back from Rome by Acca.

The Cross in the Sky

Scotland was invaded about the time of the seventh century by an English king called Athelstane.

The army, from an area of England called Anglia, camped at a place now called Athelstaneford, a village near Haddington, in East Lothian.

King Angus' army was also camped nearby, waiting for the battle to begin.

But Angus' army were very tired and the king was worried that he might lose the battle which was to take place the next day.

Eventually, worn out and very weary, Angus fell into a deep sleep.

It was then that he had a dream, a very powerful dream. For he dreamt that Saint Andrew himself appeared before him, promising the king that he would win a glorious victory in the battle which was soon to begin.

King Angus awoke full of joy. He told his commanding officers what he had seen. They too grew very excited and relieved. They thought it was a good omen.

So they told all their soldiers about it. The word spread. The men began to cheer. Saint Andrew himself had told them that they would win the battle.

They stopped feeling tired. They stopped feeling uneasy. They became filled with hope.

They became brave again. They were ready to fight well. They believed they had Saint Andrew on their side.

And then another strange thing happened.

Just as the battle began, a huge white cross-shape appeared in the sky – like vapour-trails from modern jet aircraft. It stood out boldly against the blue sky.

It was just like the 'X'-shaped cross upon which Saint Andrew had been crucified in Greece all those centuries ago.

The English army watched in awe and grew very afraid. The Picts and Scots wasted no time and launched a fierce attack. They were now sure that their saint – *Saint Andrew* – would protect them. They believed that he would lead them to victory.

They won the battle that day.

Angus believed it was the work of Saint Andrew. In gratitude he decided to give a tenth part of *all* his wealth to honour Saint Andrew. And by making sure that churches were dedicated to this saint – and lots of dedications were made in his honour – Andrew became a very familiar and important name to the people of Scotland.

★ ★ ★

There is another version to this story.

It tells us that King Angus was out walking with seven of his dearest friends when a light from Heaven shone around them. They were so afraid and in awe of the light that they fell on their faces.

A voice from Heaven came down to them, saying that this was the voice of Saint Andrew, the Apostle, who had been sent to guard and to defend King Angus.

It was foretold that the king would see the sign of the Cross in the sky and should march forward against his enemies.

The voice also said that King Angus should offer a tenth part of his wealth to honour Saint Andrew on this earth.

King Angus and his friends were astonished, but three days later the king divided his army into twelve companies or groups.

His soldiers made banners of 'X'-shaped crosses, like the one Andrew said would appear in the sky. The soldiers carried these crosses at the head of each company and a light from Heaven shone from the head of each cross.

King Angus' army won the battle.

* * *

And so we have at least two versions of this particular ancient tale. There may be other, similar, tales, involving other kings in other countries, but the important things to remember here are:
- King Angus believed that Saint Andrew was helping him.
- The king's soldiers believed that Saint Andrew was helping them.
- The king did own relics which he believed were those of Saint Andrew, although they may not have been.
- He did win the battle.
- *And it all led to Scotland having its own flag. It helped to unify Scotland as a nation.*

THINGS TO DO

- Draw the army of King Angus MacFergus looking up at the huge Cross against the blue sky.

  Or draw Saint Andrew appearing to King Angus in his dream.

  Or design your own 'X'-cross banner. Remember to make it big and bold – it had to be seen by the soldiers at the back of the lines of marching men.

- If possible, arrange a school or family visit to Athelstaneford.

  There is a memorial at Athelstaneford to the battle. It tells the story of the Saltire.

  [When the weather fades the flag which flies at the memorial, the flag is replaced. Some visitors from overseas have asked if they might take the old flag home with them. Now the old flags are flown outside people's houses in countries as far away from Scotland as Canada and Australia.]

THE ORDER OF THE THISTLE

Do you know what 'chivalry' is?

Long ago, kings and queens sometimes rewarded people who had helped them by inviting them to become part of a special organisation. These organisations were called 'Orders'.

People liked belonging to these 'Orders'. It showed others that they were high up in the favour of the king or queen. It meant that everyone knew they were important. Sometimes they even had special uniforms to wear, or badges or medals.

One of these Orders had an early connection with Saint Andrew. How did this come about?

The oldest Order in Scotland is called the 'Order of the Thistle'. Legend says that it was founded in the eighth century by a king called Achaius. He set it up after he had won a battle against invading Saxons from south of the border. He wanted to celebrate his victory and to honour some of the soldiers who had fought bravely for him.

But some historians say this Order may not have been founded by Achaius at all. They say that King James V of Scotland began this very famous Order in 1540 and, to begin with, it was called the 'Order of Saint Andrew'.

But the early Order of Saint Andrew was not used very often by some later kings and it fell into disuse. It was not until 1687 that King James VII (James II of England) awarded it again under the title of the 'Order of the Thistle'. It still flourishes today.

HOLY DAYS

Nearly every home and office has a calendar showing the months of the year and dates for every day. Long ago the calendar had particular days linked to saints. On that day people would go to church or remember to honour a saint in a special way. Today the word 'holiday' comes from this tradition. On a 'holy day' the people did not have to work, but instead attended church or celebrated a saint's day in some other way. Some countries still hold colourful processions, fairs or markets on particular saints' days. And some of the most important dates are called feast days, because people used to hold a celebration meal on that day.

The 30th of November is Saint Andrew's Day.

Some Scottish businesses, colleges and local authority buildings fly the Saltire flag that day. An organisation called the Saltire Society, which was set up to encourage Scottish culture, has started a campaign to get more businesses and organisations to fly the Scottish flag. In some other countries, like Norway or the United States, it is normal to fly the national flag on public buildings, on people's houses, or in their gardens, all year round.

Have you also noticed that football and rugby fans around the world have started painting the Saltire or other national flags on their faces?

November 30th is a special day for Scottish people who live over-seas. They often hold Scottish events that day — like concerts with Scottish songs, or Burns Suppers to honour Scotland's famous poet, Robert Burns. It is interesting also that Scotland is not the only country which honours Andrew as a Patron Saint. Romania, Greece and Russia also claim Andrew as their special saint.

THE SALTIRE

- Long ago, banners or flags which showed pictures of saints also became used as the banners or flags of whole nations.
- In 1286, the Great Seal of the Guardians of Scotland – those nobles and leaders who looked after Scotland after the death of a monarch and before the crowning of a new ruler, or when the new monarch was only a child – included the figure of Saint Andrew.
- In 1385, when a Scottish army was preparing to invade England, the Scots Parliament decreed that every man should wear the white Saint Andrew 'X'-shaped Cross on his armour.
- Scots who went to fight in the Crusades from the eleventh to the thirteenth centuries – the campaigns to free the Holy Land from Arab and Moslem armies (see page 64) – carried banners showing the Saltire.
- The figure of Saint Andrew and his Saltire Cross appeared on Scottish coins, wax seals and badges long ago.
- Sometimes ancient map-makers in other countries would put a shield or banner or coat-of-arms on their maps to illustrate a country. Scotland was often represented by the Saltire.
- Scottish ships long ago flew the Saltire flag, and ports and harbours also carried it on their banners, flags and coats-of-arms.
- Scottish soldiers who joined the armies of other rulers in other countries, as allies or paid warriors (known as mercenaries), often include the Saltire on their uniforms, flags or badges. Scottish regiments did the same.
- Many modern Scottish companies, banks, universities, colleges and other organisations have the Saltire in their coat-of-arms.

CHAPTER 5

Patron Saints
of the U.K.

SCOTLAND is the only country in the United Kingdom to have

one of the Apostles, one of the first followers of Jesus, as a Patron Saint. But the others countries in the United Kingdom have some equally interesting individuals as their Patron Saints.

England – Saint George

George was a martyr who died for his faith in Jesus Christ. He is thought – like Andrew – to have been killed because he preached Christianity to people who were not very happy to hear this powerful message. George may have been killed at a place called Lydda in Palestine. He died in AD 303 and people celebrate a feast day in his honour on the 23rd of April – Saint George's Day.

George was a very well known saint among Christians for six hundred years. This was before the much-loved tale of George slaying a dragon became familiar in the twelfth century.

The dragon story tells how a king's daughter was about to be sacrificed to a monster. [This king may have reigned in the Middle East, possible in one of the countries we call Libya or Syria.]

George, wearing his knight's armour, first captured the dragon. He then said to the people that if they believed in Jesus and were baptised ('christened'), then he would *kill* the dragon. Thousands became Christians at once, so George slew the dragon. He then returned the princess to her father and the king was delighted.

This legend may not be true. There is a similar story from Ancient Greece which tells of a handsome warrior, called Perseus, who could fly. He rescued a beautiful princess, Andromeda, by killing a sea monster.

There is also an old Celtic legend from Scotland which tells of a Christian knight called Martin who rescued a farmer's daughters from a monster near a place called Pitempton, near Dundee.

★ ★ ★

King Richard the Lionheart of England is said to have had a vision of Saint George. [Perhaps this may seem very similar to King Angus MacFergus and his vision of the Saltire in the night sky on pages 53 to 55.] After the vision, Richard restored an old church at Lydda (also called Diospolis), which was believed to have contained the bones of Saint George.

In the days of King Richard, the special and holy places in Palestine – the Holy Land, where Jesus had lived, walked and taught – had become Christian shrines. However, they were in danger of being overrun by armies who were not Christian. These armies of Moslem, Turkish and Arab warriors were called Saracens.

King Richard organised armies of English soldiers to fight the Saracens. These campaigns and battles were called the Crusades.

Richard's men also had a vision during the Crusades. The city of Jerusalem was being besieged by the Crusaders when Saint George suddenly appeared in a vision. He wore white with a red cross on his breast. The soldiers believed that George then led them up ladders on to the city walls and so helped the soldiers to capture the city.

This particular story helped to make George the Patron Saint of England, but a similar story is told involving the city of Antioch instead of Jerusalem.

Lots of Scots in past centuries did not like Saint George, because Scotland and England were often at war. If the Scots saw soldiers wearing white garments with the red cross of Saint George on it, they knew they were facing the 'auld enemy'.

The English kings, Edward I and II, when they tried to conquer Scotland in the thirteenth and fourteenth centuries, had the Saint George's Cross flown on their ships.

And when King James VI of Scotland also became King James I of England in 1603, at the Union of the Crowns, he asked his sailors to join up, to intertwine, the Saint Andrew Cross of Scotland and the Saint George Cross of England and to fly the joint flag on their main masts.

The Cross of Saint George, with the Union Flag tucked away in one corner, is still flown as the 'White Ensign', the flag of the British Royal Navy. However, strictly speaking, this should not have happened. When Scotland and England joined up at the Treaty of Union in 1707, a new flag for the new *British* Navy was to be designed. It never happened.

Ireland – Saint Patrick

Patrick is the Patron Saint of Ireland. It is thought that his father may have been a Roman official who lived in Britain. Patrick was born in Britain, but scholars differ as to where that might have been. Dumbarton in Strathclyde is one suggestion.

It is believed that Patrick was captured by Irish raiders and taken to Northern Ireland as a slave. He became a Christian there.

Many churches, towns and cities all over Ireland have links with Patrick, but there may have been another saint, also called Patrick, and the two men might have been mixed up by some historians.

It is thought that Patrick may have visited France and other areas of mainland Europe. And he may have travelled and taught in Britain. But nearly all his main links are with Ireland and he is greatly honoured in Ireland to this day and by Irish communities all over the world.

Patrick was a great missionary for Christianity, a wonderful preacher and bishop. He lived, it is thought, from about AD 390-461 and his feast day is on the 17th of March.

Wales – Saint David

David is the Patron Saint of Wales. His name in the Welsh language is *Dewi Sant*. It is thought that he may have been the son of a Welsh chief. He was born on the Cardigan coast of Wales at a place called Mynyw (called *Menevia* in Latin). It is spelt today as 'Henfynw'. He died in either AD 509 or 601 – accounts vary – and his feast day is on the 1st of March.

David was a great Christian missionary who set up communities for work and worship. One of these became known as *Yy Ddewi* – 'David's House'. This community became a small, cathedral city now known as St David's.

David's name is often spelt as 'Dafydd', pronounced 'Daffid'. The nickname 'Taffy' for a Welshmen comes from this word.

★ ★ ★

There is also a Scottish saint called David – King David I (c.1080-1153), the youngest son of King Malcolm Canmore III, known as Malcolm 'Bighead' (meaning 'great' or 'noble' perhaps) and Saint Margaret of Scotland (see page 48). David supported the building of

many of Scotland's great abbeys and cathedrals. He is buried in
Dunfermline and his feast day is on the 24th of May.

★ ★ ★

Many centuries ago Scotland and England fought against each other
because English rulers wanted to conquer Scotland as they had con-
quered Wales.

But the Scots wanted their nation to be independent of English
rule. And so they fought many battles. One particular Battle in 1314
was fought at Bannockburn near Stirling. The Scots won that day.

But to ensure the future safety and independence of Scotland,
the Scots wrote to the Pope in Rome, seeking his help.

The Pope at that time was a man called John XXII. When priests
or cardinals were appointed as Pope, they took another name, gen-
erally the name of one of Jesus' Disciples or some other holy figure.
This meant that Pope John XXII (22nd) was the 22nd Pope to
take the particular name of John.

Pope John was head of the Catholic Church and held a lot of
power. Indeed, sometimes he acted like a one-man United Nations,
telling countries what to do and how to do it!

The Scots wanted Pope John to tell all future English Kings to
leave Scotland alone. But the English wanted him to support their
claims to possess Scotland as part of their country.

The Scots wrote a famous letter to the Pope in the year 1320. It
is now called the 'Declaration of Arbroath', because it was written
at a meeting of the Scottish Parliament held at Arbroath.

It is a famous declaration of freedom.

It is a famous declaration of liberty.

It is a famous declaration of nationhood.

At one point in this letter the Scots remind the Pope that Saint Andrew is their Patron Saint. It says:

'Our Lord Jesus Christ, who is the King of Kings, called them among the first to His most firm faith, after His Passion and Resurrection … '

The letter here is saying that the Scots were early Christians. Christ's 'Passion and Resurrection' means that Jesus died on the Cross so that everyone might have the chance to know and to worship God in a new and special way. It means that Jesus rose from the dead and then went to Heaven. The letter goes on …

'Nor did He choose to confirm them in the Lord's Faith by any one less than His own first Apostle (although he stands second or third in order of rank), the most gracious Andrew, brother of Peter's self, whomever since He has established their Patron … '

In this way the Scots reminded Pope John that the Apostle Andrew is Scotland's Patron Saint. And they reminded the Pope that Andrew is Peter's brother.

The letter goes on to say that earlier Popes had protected Scotland and had granted Scotland many favours. One of the reasons they had done this was because Scotland 'belonged' to Peter's brother, Andrew. Peter was considered to be the first Pope of all, by the Roman Catholic Church

THINGS TO DO

- The 'Declaration of Arbroath' is one of the most important documents in Scotland's history. Perhaps you can find a copy in a history book to read. Or try to read a copy of the original – the writing is quite difficult, but worth the effort.
  [There is a modern booklet, by the distinguished historian and former newspaper editor and managing editor James S. Adam, which shows the 'Declaration of Arbroath' in the languages of Latin, English, Scots and Gaelic.]
- Make a model or draw a picture of the Scottish noblemen attaching their family seals to the 'Declaration'.
- Do you know where Arbroath is?
  Look it up on a map of Scotland.

A Prayer For Saint Andrew

Help us to love our land,
but to hate no other.

Help us to love and appreciate
our own traditions,
but to understand and respect
the beliefs of others.

Help us bring love and understanding
where there is hate
and distrust.

Protect this nation, Scotland,
and all who live here
and to make the Cross of Scotland
a symbol of love, friendship, hope,
justice and compassion.

Saint Andrew, pray for us.

The Dumyat Trilogy

In *The Day the Mountain Moved,* Gavin and his friends, fresh from *Light on Dumyat* and *The White Stag Adventure,* go back in time to face the 'good' and 'bad' figures of Scottish Celtic mythology.

Light on Dumyat was chosen for a primary schools conference at Stirling University, *The White Stag Adventure* was broadcast by BBC for schools, and *The Day the Mountain Moved* reached the Scottish Top Ten Books. All three books are used in Scottish schools.

Robert Burns for Beginners

'A much-needed book … McOwan's DIY Burns Supper is designed to enthuse children with the fun of the evening without neglecting its more serious side …'
SCOTLAND ON SUNDAY

'The sort of book that makes young readers comfortable with poetry and makes it a natural part of their culture.' BOOKS IN SCOTLAND

Young people studying the work of ROBERT BURNS find few specially-produced volumes to work from. Included in this book is an introduction to the life of Robert Burns; samples of his poetry and songs; advice and instructions on how to organise a Burns Supper – plus project suggestions for class and individual participation.

[All titles available from Saint Andrew Press, 121 George Street, Edinburgh EH2 4YN – Tel: 0131 225 5722]

Other books by
Rennie McOwan